Unpredictable Circumstances

Wilfred Fisher

VANTAGE PRESS
New York

FIRST EDITION

All rights reserved, including the right of
reproduction in whole or in part in any form.

Copyright © 1998 by Wilfred Fisher

Published by Vantage Press, Inc.
516 West 34th Street, New York, New York 10001

Manufactured in the United States of America
ISBN: 0-533-12672-X

Library of Congress Catalog Card No.: 97-091436

0 9 8 7 6 5 4 3 2 1

1

As a kid, Michael was shy. He grew up the oldest of three kids, in a family-oriented atmosphere filled with love and affection. His father was an ex-marine, who had fought in the Vietnam War; now, he is working as an electrical engineer. A trade he had learned while in the marines, and later continued to pursue by later returning back to school and receiving his bachelor's degree in engineering. Michael's mother was a housewife for most of her son's life; she stayed at home taking care of the family. As her three kids got older, she returned to the job market with hardly any experience, but with her struggles and determination, she was able to find an entry-level job as a receptionist. With many years of hard work and perseverance, she was able to advance and move up in rank. All of her hard work paid off by later receiving the title of supervisor for the company she worked for. She put in many hours of work a week and she was also able to maintain the amount of hours that she needed to spend with her family. Her kids appreciated the hours and love that their mom showed for them.

Growing up in this family was a tremendous experience for Michael. He was a stubborn individual. Someone who did as he believed to be right. He was a leader. He always followed his beliefs, through this process, he made many mistakes, but learned from each and every one. He was taught to accept the outcome of his decisions and to stand by them and to take them as they were presented to him. Michael lived by this saying. Even though he and his father didn't have the best of relationships, as far as communication was concerned, there was a mutual respect between them. Michael always thought highly of his father, he bragged about his father to his peers. His father had no idea as to how much he spoke or thought of him. That would have definitely made his father proud to know of his son's feelings for him.

In April of 1989, Michael had gone to his father to let him know of his decision to join the Navy, and due to the fact that his father had Armed Forces Services experience, he did not agree with Michael's decision. He wanted him to go to college and to take advantage of the educational system.

Michael's father thought of his son's future as changing, he believed that an education would be essential in his son's generation. He did not see any greater accomplishment, other than seeing his son receive a college degree. But at that time, Michael did not see it that way. He felt he needed to go away from his surroundings to find out more about himself. This is when he resorted to joining a branch of the armed forces.

Michael's individuality played an important part in his decision to join the services. His stubborn ways prompted him to join the Navy and to go against what his father had suggested. So, the following month, May third, 1989, he decided to sign up for four years of active service in the Navy. But, he was not scheduled to depart for three months.

2

On the morning of August 17, 1989, Michael Guthridge headed toward the MEPS station Fort Hamilton on the south side of Brookyn, NY. He was determined to get away and fulfill his four years of service commitment to the government, hoping for the best without knowing anything of what was to face him ahead.

There he was, on the MEPS station sitting, waiting for his orders. He was to be taken to Trenton, New Jersey, to begin boot camp, in preparation for his Naval career. Boot camp was to take twelve weeks of hard training and discipline. While at boot camp, Michael found it the hardest to adapt to taking orders from all kinds of individuals. This was a new experience for him and he wanted to succeed really badly. So he learned to tolerate the orders and discipline that he found himself receiving.

This was his first experience away from home; he took it well, as this was his big break from all the pressures that he felt his family was putting on him. Later, he realized that the pressure was nothing compared to the pressure put on him by the military. He had a set schedule; the time to wake each and every morning was determined for him, as well as a set time for eating and everything else that you can possibly imagine was pre-planned. All he had to do was go through the motions of each day.

In boot camp, each day began at 4:30 A.M., at which time all he had time to do was to put on his clothes for the day, fix his bed and take care of his personal hygiene in preparation for that day's inspection. By 5:00 A.M., his squadron was out onto the fields for their daily drilling exercises, which lasted approximately one hour. Then they would return back to the barracks in preparation for the morning breakfast.

His squadron would automatically head down to the cafeteria for breakfast, at approximately 6:30 A.M. Breakfast was only ten minutes, so, he found himself having to eat at a very fast rate. After breakfast, they would have a few minutes to refresh and take care of their personal hygiene, once again.

As the morning went along, they would have classes scheduled. They would vary day by day, at times they might have to go to the shooting range to shoot a few rounds, by the time all of these activities were finished, it would be time for the afternoon's lunch. The squadron would head back to the cafeteria for their lunch, this was no different than the morning's breakfast, where they had ten minutes to eat all of their food.

After lunch, it was back to drills, marching, running, exercising, or taking care of some sort of paper work. It would all depend on that day's schedule. By 5:30 P.M., it was time for dinner, so, the squadron would head back to the cafeteria for the day's last meal.

By 6:00 P.M., they were back in the barracks, taking care of their laundry, studying, taking showers, and getting ready for the next day.

At 9:00 P.M., it was everyone's best time of the day, for it was time for the mail call and letter writing. It was a better time for those who had mail coming in, than for those who had no one writing them. In the case of Michael, he had a few friends who would keep in contact by writing him. His girlfriend Adrian would also write at times. He felt special every time he received a letter, but he would feel extra special and more inclined to want to read it, when it was from Adrian. He saw Adrian as being his Angel, his star. He cherished the floor this lady walked on. He was in love with her and the feeling was mutual on her behalf. Adrian thought of no one but Michael and Michael thought of no one but Adrian. All he could do was think of returning home to spend some time with his Angel.

There were times when the squadron received a few minutes to call their loved ones and he wasted no time in calling Adrian to inquire about her well-being. If she was not home, he would be disappointed and take that opportunity to call his family. This routine went on for the 12 weeks that Michael was in boot camp. The only day that the routine was any different, was on Sundays; when it was time to go to church for those who wanted to go. It was also time for relaxation and to take time to get to know his other fellow Navy men.

On November 10th, 1989, Michael graduated from boot camp. He took two weeks off before having to head out for military training school. These two weeks off, couldn't have come any sooner or at a better time for Michael, for his girlfriend's birthday was on November 22nd. After his two weeks off, he was to head down to Jacksonville, Florida for school. He was to study about radars and alarms.

On Friday November 22nd, 1989, Michael planned to spend the entire evening with his lady. He made reservations for them to have dinner together in a luxury hotel which he had selected prior to returning back home. The couple stayed up all night to watch the moon. Neither one of them wanted to waste any time, they were trying to spend as much time together as the night would allow them to have. Knowing that New York and Florida are a long distance apart, and that the only way of communicating would be via a telephone.

On the evening of November 24th, Adrian dropped Michael at Kennedy International Airport, where he was to head down to Florida. His plane was to depart at 6:00 P.M. that evening. Minutes after arriving at the airport, Adrian gave Michael a bye-bye kiss, at which time they both started to cry, and swore to each other to remain in each other's thoughts forever. The plane ride took approximately 2 hours, it was a short trip. From the airport, he took a taxi cab to his new command. He reported to barracks 89, where he was to be stationed for the next six months before heading out to his permanent duty station. The first chance Michael received after arriving in Florida, he ensured that he called Adrian to let her know of his well-being.

While at school, he focused more on where he was going to be stationed permanently; he wanted to select a location that would be close to his love, Adrian. His expectations were high, he didn't think that anything could go wrong. He had a strong belief, that he was going to get an opportunity to be stationed close to Adrian. In this case it would be Richmond, Virginia.

So, when he was asked, to decide on a geographical location, there was no hesitation on his selecting Virginia. He saw Richmond as being only a five hour drive away from his home town of Brooklyn, NY, and an hour away if he were to take the plane.

Obviously, Richmond, Virginia was a logical choice for Michael. But, meanwhile, he had to focus on attending school. He knew that receiving good grades in school, would actually increase his chances of getting the duty station he had wished for all this time. The military had a policy of allowing the students with the best grades to have first choice when selecting a duty station. He focused himself into his studies, and he had a weekly test. Michael would normally score the highest grades on the weekly test. His work at school did not go unnoticed. His instructors took notice and they vowed to grant him his wish, for his hard work. So, after completion of school, Michael received his wish. He was granted Richmond, Virginia, as his new permanent duty station. This was the station he was to stay at until the ending of his contract.

He took this opportunity to buy a car and it did not take him long before he owned his car. He went to the credit union and requested a loan that was granted to him within two days. This was a joyous occasion for Michael. He bought his car and already found himself making plans to go home on the following weekend to see his love, Adrian.

Now, it was almost one year since he had joined the military and he couldn't wait until he was discharged from the military. Going out on the field and working long hours was getting to him.

He thought of himself as drifting away from his love, Adrian. It came to the point where he was not communicating with her on a regular basis, and he found himself worrying and wondering about his relationship status. But he had such a great woman by his side that she found the way to assure him of the safety of their relationship. Michael felt secured after hearing his Angel assure him of their relationship. He was then able to focus once again on his Naval career.

He went through some long months of hard and constant training; they would get up early each morning and conduct their training for long hours each day. Michael was going through the motions and nothing seemed to bother him. Because of Adrian's assurance, he did not let anything or anyone get to him. This process went on for about a year, by this time he had already completed two years of service, half the amount of time he needed to accomplish his commitment to the Navy.

3

On the morning of September 24, 1991, Michael was sleeping when he felt two guards attempting to wake him up to be arrested. He was baffled because he had no idea as to why he was being arrested. He was taken into custody without any explanations as to why he was being arrested.

As the day went along, he came to find out that he was arrested for larceny and unlawful entry into a storeroom on base. He had no idea as to what they were talking about. He was insisting on his innocence, but they did not believe anything that he was saying. Michael's word was irrelevant; he was framed by another individual, who gave the guards Michael's name. A man by the name of Stanley Jackson was responsible for Michael's arrest. He had accused him of all this doing. Michael had no idea that this individual had framed him. He had later found out from his lawyer who had told him the reason for his arrest. He was being detained while an investigation was taking place. While this investigation took place, Michael had no choice, but to sit tight and wait to see the outcome of this nightmare.

The military was fearful of letting him go free, they feared that he would leave the state if released. Michael had no reason to leave the state because he was not guilty of any crime.

While in the brig, he met other inmates, who were there for other crimes. He met a man by the name of Roger Henderson who was in the brig for attempting to explode a building, it seems that Roger was very good with explosives. They would talk about their experiences, Michael told him about his innocence and that he was framed. He had also mentioned to him that he was familiar with radars and alarms because he had been taking that as a trade in the military. Roger told Michael the reason for him being in the brig. He explained to him, that he had tried to destroy a financial institution because of the military withholding his checks. Apparently, someone had made a mistake when they were distributing the checks which was the reason for Roger not receiving his checks. He was desperate for money because he was behind on a lot of bills. As time went along, both men became closer to each other. They later started to confide in each other. Roger was sentenced to do five years, four of which he has already served, he was scheduled for release in June of 1992. Michael was still awaiting a decision based on the ongoing investigation. The investigators did not find anything to indict or acquit him, so, they had planned to keep him in the brig until something developed. Through all these tribulations, Adrian was still on Michael's side, and so was Roger's wife. It was like the more these two men talked, the more things they found in common about themselves.

Life in the brig was no different than in the Navy, with the exception that you do not get a chance to go home. In the brig, they still had to get up early each morning, there were three meals each day, as well as a set time to go to sleep. They also had a job to perform while in the brig. Both men had to cut grass everyday for eight hours each day. Jobs in the brig varied, it just happened that both of these men received the same assignment of cutting grass. Basically, in the brig each day was planned. In his spare time, Michael played cards and he also found himself reading a lot of different books because they did have a library and he had a lot of time to spare.

It was a coincidence, that a month later, on the 22 of November, 1991, he was scheduled to appear in court. That day just happened to be his girlfriend's birthday. So, early that morning, he was escorted to the courtroom by two guards. In the courtroom, the judge, the prosecutor, the defense lawyer, the two guards, the stenographer and Michael were the only individuals present inside of the courtroom. Michael was given an option, as to whom he wanted presiding over his case, and after his lawyer had advised him, he decided that it would be in his best interest to have the judge and not a panel of jurors. Due to the fact that if the judge was the only individual presiding over this case, it was supposed to or expected to take a long time.

Officially, the court hearing got under way at approximately 9:00 A.M., this was the time that the judge had officially entered the courtroom and it was announced that he would be presiding over this case. This was the case of the U.S. Navy vs. Michael Guthridge. The charges were read; he had two charges against him, one of larceny and the other one was unlawful entry.

Michael's command had offered his lawyer a deal, they wanted her client to plead guilty and they would consider his time spent in the brig as sufficient time spent and he would be released the same day of his court hearing. Michael wanted no part of that, he did not think he should do any time for a crime he did not commit. But after reconsidering with the help of his lawyer, he started to weigh his options. He knew that, he could be released immediately upon his acceptance of the Navy's offer. He did not know whether to take a chance of a guilty finding and having to do years or take the chance of being found guilty and go home. The sound of not guilty sounded good to Michael because of his innocence but at the same time, he did not want to take a chance of being found guilty and do years for something he did not commit. Michael was advised by his lawyer to exercise his options.

At the time of the hearing, he still had not made up his

mind. After his lawyer's advice, he took his fifth amendment right, and remained quiet throughout the trial. So, when asked, by the judge, he followed his lawyer's advice and remained quiet. Michael knew of his innocence, even though, they believed him to be guilty of both charges.

After listening to the trial and seeing the direction the trial was going, Michael did not like his chances. It felt to him, as if they were out to get him for an indescribable reason. So, after carefully listening to the case for about 45 minutes, both lawyers made their closing statements, at which time, the judge had asked to be excused to conduct his deliberation of the case.

During this time, Michael started feeling the heat and the thought of not seeing his Angel for a couple of years triggered in his mind. He changed his mind and asked his lawyer to take the offer the Navy was giving him if it was still available. At first, his lawyer was skeptical about him changing his plea, she believed that she had the case won, because of insufficient evidence against Michael, but even though, he did not want to take the chance of being found guilty. So, his lawyer complied with Michael's wish and after speaking with the prosecutor, she agreed to change her not guilty plea to guilty. All they had to do, was sign the agreement papers and explain the happenings to the judge, once he returned from deliberations.

Once the judge heard of all the changes, he agreed to the change of plea. He granted Michael his release from the brig under the conditions stated on the agreement, which he signed in the presence of his lawyer. Along with the agreement, Michael was also discharged from the military with a bad conduct discharge. He was fined a 500 dollars fine and reduced in rank from E-4 to E-1. To Michael all of that was irrelevant, he was the happiest guy in the world, he saw himself as getting his wish, even though he had to accept a plea of guilty to receive his release from the brig. He saw this as an opportunity to return home and start his life over. His girlfriend, Adrian, saw this as the best birthday gift she could have received, because she did not want to see Michael remain in the brig. Now, both of them were very optimistic about a future together.

Prior to leaving the brig, Michael ensured that he said goodbye to some of the friends he had made. In particular, Roger. He said good-bye to his good friend and left his phone number and address so Roger could keep in contact with him. Both parties made a promise to keep a good communication.

The rest of the day, was devoted to taking care of paper work; the faster he took care of his paper work, would mean a faster release from the brig. To his surprise, his lawyer had taken care of everything. All he had to do, was sign a few papers and head back home to Brooklyn, NY.

4

The next day, Michael flew back home, his family was anxiously awaiting his return. They planned a party and celebrated along with his girlfriend. Michael must have been the happiest man in the world on this day. His girlfriend couldn't have been any happier to see a smile on her man's face. He was surrounded by all his loved ones. He had his family and the woman he loved, who stood by him through all his adversities. Michael was a lucky individual to have all this many people care for him.

Later on this evening, Michael and Adrian sneaked out of the party without anyone noticing. He wanted to be alone with Adrian, so, they could celebrate her birthday together. She was so happy to be next to her man, knowing that he would not have to return back to the military. But to her surprise, Michael had another surprise for her. He proposed and she ecstatically accepted. Adrian could not think of anything to say. She was shocked to hear this from Michael, she thought of this day as being the highlight of her life. A day after her birthday and having the man she loved propose to her, she had a dream that she was pregnant and she could not wait to tell Michael, even though she knew it was only a dream. Everything just seemed to be going their way, they had planned to get married in the summer of 1992.

Adrian could not wait to share her news with her family. After sharing the news, her parents were delighted to know that Michael and their daughter were getting married in the summer. They could not think of a happier occasion than giving their daughter away to this lovely man. They thought very highly of Michael, they treated him as one of their own. Adrian had a brother who was also delighted to hear about his sister's scheduled wedding. He was also close to Michael, as he saw him as the older brother figure he never had. Adrian's family was so happy about this news, that they made plans to have the Guthridge family join them for a New Year's dinner.

The soon to be married couple spent all their time together, as they were trying to make up for lost time. Even though they were together on a regular basis, they kept everything in perspective. Michael knew that he had to find a job. He was hoping that it would be something in radar or alarms, since, he had prior experience in those areas. As for Adrian, she had a degree in business, but, she found herself having difficulties in finding a job related to her field. She was working as a legal secretary for a firm. She was hoping to gain valuable experience, while she worked on getting a job that she believed to be related to business. Michael was lucky to find a job two weeks prior to Christmas, as a car alarm installer, a job he felt would carry him through the holidays. This job would help him save enough money to have his dream wedding in the summer.

Michael and his fiancée were together on Christmas Eve. At 12:00 A.M., Christmas Day, he officially proposed by giving her a ring he was able to buy, with the money he earned from his recent job. But to Michael's surprise, Adrian had even greater news to inform him of, she told him that she was a month pregnant. He was delighted to hear of this news.

Michael thought, he was living in a fairy tale, everything just seemed to have been going his way, after things seemed to be going bad in the military. First, he was released from the brig, after being accused of a crime he did not commit, then he was discharged from the military. After returning home, he proposed to his girlfriend, he later found out about his new job, and now he was told that he was an expecting father. Michael just felt good to know that everything was going his way for a change. Michael and Adrian planned on waiting until the New Year's dinner to inform the rest of the family.

On New Year's Day, the Guthridge family went over to the Griffey family house for dinner. This was time for the families to come together as one, there was mutual respect and a lot of love to spread around. The two main people for whom the family was having the dinner for, were still not at the dinner. Michael and Adrian were delaying their presence at the party, in anticipation of creating enough suspense before informing the rest of the family of their expecting a newborn baby.

An hour into the dinner, Michael and Adrian made their entrance into the house and everyone was happy to see the couple. They wasted no time in letting everyone know that they were expecting their first child. Both families were elated to hear of the news. They were getting used to hearing good news from the young couple and also the family were all happy for their new found happiness. The family hoped and prayed that their happiness could last, and before the night ended, they made a toast in honor of the soon to be married couple and expecting parents.

Michael and Adrian had made a promise not to move in together until after the wedding. So, life went as usual for the couple. They saw each other every day, and all they could talk about was the wedding.

Preparations started to take place in anticipation for a huge wedding, but they first had to agree on a wedding date. The logical choice was June 14, 1992, since they had gone on their first date on that day seven years ago. This was to be a very magical day. They were surprised to see that they were still together after seven years of up and down battles. They did not think that anyone or any adversity could possibly separate them after all that they had been through. They had started making their guest list, they were expecting at least 500 guests. They were also expecting relatives to come from all over the country, even as far as California; Michael had relatives over there. In particular his cousin Veronica, whom he included in the wedding's activities. He loved her as his own sister.

Michael found himself having to work many shifts, he tried to put in enough hours to save enough money for the wedding. Adrian was not too fond of the idea of Michael working double shifts because she was not able to see him as often as she was accustomed to. She was able to quickly adapt, because, she knew that he was doing all of this for them, so, she was very sympathetic of his actions.

Michael knew that she would understand because that was just the type of individual that his fiancée was, very understanding. This hard work went on for about four months, and he stopped a month prior to the wedding. As the date drew closer, anticipation kept building. Michael did not want Adrian to participate too much in the wedding's preparation. All of this was due to the fact that, by this time she was six months pregnant and he did not want to put too much pressure on her or on the baby. He was overprotective of her, he only cared about her well being. That was the single most important thing in his life. As long as Adrian was happy, he found himself happy. As Adrian would always do, Michael always put his family ahead, that being Adrian and his unborn baby.

A week prior to the wedding, Michael found an apartment. This was to be the new home for his family. With the help of his and his fiancée's parents, he was able to purchase enough furniture to furnish the apartment. He was going to move in after the honeymoon. He wanted to move at the same time as his wife. That was the reason for him waiting until after the honeymoon.

The day prior to the wedding, some of Michael's friends had gathered together and surprised him with a bachelor's party. But Michael was even more surprised to see his old friend Roger at the party. He had just completed the final year of his five year sentence. Michael took the opportunity to thank him for showing up at the party. He tried to catch up on old times.

But Roger insisted on Michael focusing more on his big day. Roger was happy to see Michael as well, he gave him his phone number and told him that they could catch up on old times, once he returned from his honeymoon. Michael was elated to see all of his friends share this happy moment with him, he thanked them all and praised them for being such good friends.

5

On the morning of the wedding, Adrian woke up and tried to do a million things at once, so her mother had to slow her down. She was anxious to get this day over with, she wanted to be Mrs. Guthridge. Over at his house, Michael was more at ease. Even though he was as nervous as Adrian, he tried not to show it, and tried to maintain a cool and collective attitude. The wedding was scheduled for 10:00 A.M., Michael was at the church at 9:00 A.M., and the bride had not arrived. She was still at home, getting ready for her big day. All of the guests were at church in anticipation of this wedding. The bride arrived at the church at a quarter to ten. She thought she would be late for her own wedding.

The ceremony started to get under way at exactly 10:00 A.M., which surprised many people. The bishop went ahead and started the ceremony as he welcomed everyone at the church. He said a few prayers and by 10:40 A.M., the couple were exchanging vows. He first asked him, "would you Michael Guthridge take this woman to be your wife," and he quickly replied, "yes I do." Adrian was then asked the same question, and without any hesitation, she said, "yes I do," "I love you, I love you, Michael Guthridge," then the bishop pronounced them as husband wife. They wasted no time in kissing each other, they were so happy to be married to each other. The couple skipped the reception and quickly headed to the airport to start their honeymoon. They had reservations to fly down to Florida where they were to take a cruise to some islands that included the Bahamas, St. Thomas and Puerto Rico. The cruise was to last a week. After arriving in Florida, they took a charter bus that took them straight to the pier where the ship was scheduled to depart.

Once they got settled on the ship, they headed to the dining room for a romantic dinner. After dinner, they went out to get a good look at the sea, where they could appreciate each other's company. While out at sea, Michael catered to all of Adrian's needs. He never left her side and stayed by her throughout the entire week, knowing that she was pregnant. He feared that if he left her side, she would need something and he would not be able to help her out. Michael was gracious of the time they spent together. While on board the ship they danced, they ate, they went to the pool and enjoyed every moment together. They had a great time. At the completion of the cruise, they returned back to New York on the twenty-first of June.

After arriving in New York, they moved into their new apartment. They had promised to move in together after they had gotten married. Adrian was surprised because she knew nothing about the apartment, Michael along with his parents and his in-laws kept it a secret from Adrian.

Adrian was not scheduled to return to work until after her pregnancy and Michael had another week before returning to work, they only gave him two weeks vacation, due to the fact that he was new at his job, which meant he had no seniority.

Michael returned back to work a week later. Everything was going well, he just could not wait until his wife gave birth to their baby. He was fond of having to think about a name for his new baby. The doctors had already informed them that it was going to be a boy. Michael did not see it suitable to name his son to be, Jr. He wanted a new and original name for his son. Adrian had always liked Tyler, so, they figured that to be one of his names. Michael thought of Montel, so, the baby's name was to be Montel Tyler Guthridge.

6

On the eve of August 30, 1992, Adrian gave birth to their first child, it was a boy, as the doctors had predicted. It was a joyous occasion for the mother and father; having their first child. This was an unforgettable experience for Michael, who was in the delivery room, when his wife was giving birth to their newborn. Michael cried as his baby was coming out of his mother. He could not stand to see Adrian go through all of that pain. Her pain seemed to be unbearable. He could not believe how beautiful of a baby his son was. He was amazed. He was happy to know that this baby was created out of his and Adrian's love. Michael felt a strong bond to his family and promised never to leave any of them.

While Michael went to work, Adrian stayed home and cared for their baby. This baby gave Michael more of a reason to come straight home after work. He did not want to miss out on his kid's early months, he tried to be there physically and financially. Even though Michael's father was there for him financially, he was not always there physically. He always found time for his friends instead. Michael did not hold a grudge against his father because he knew deep inside that his father was a good man, he just didn't know how to express his feelings. Michael tried to be a good father to his son, he tried to be there for his son at all times. He was devoted, he tried not to make the same mistakes that his father had. He tried not to ever put his friends ahead, to prioritize, by putting his family first.

As Michael came home each and every day, he would first kiss his wife, then his son and let them both know of how much he loved them. Michael felt blessed to have a wife like Adrian caring for their child, and Adrian was happy to have a man like Michael providing them with all of their needs. Theirs was a supportive and loving family. They shared everything. Even though Montel was young, they still found the time to take him to the park, along with doing other family oriented activities, just to keep a close bond among their family.

Montel was now a year old and his parents were celebrating it with a birthday party. The turn out for the party was good. There were many kids at the party celebrating along with Montel. He was now walking and attempting to talk. He took his first steps when he was ten months old, which seemed like an eternity to Montel's parents. They were anxiously anticipating his first steps and when they first saw them, they could not wait to tell the world. This occasion along with the party made his parents proud; seeing their little boy grow up to be the big boy he is today. His first year was a big deal to his parents, just like it is for any other parents with a child.

The Guthridge family had come a long way from when they first started. Adrian still had not returned to her job and her husband was encouraging her not to. Michael was the sole provider for his family. He had assumed this role when his wife stopped working to give delivery to their baby. This was a responsibility Michael did not mind having. Adrian took the opportunity to enjoy every moment with her infant. Everything seemed to be going well for the family. The baby was healthy, Adrian was a good mother and Michael was providing the family with all of their needs.

7

On September 12 1993, the alarm shop where Michael worked, caught on fire. There was no clear reason for the fire. There were assumptions as to what created the shop to burn down. Michael was devastated to hear of the news.

Just when he thought that everything was going well, this incident happened. He was so proud of the fact that he was the sole provider of the family, but this mishap devastated him. He was not at work when this incident happened. A co-worker had called him at his house to inform him of the news. He had to break the news to his wife, which he did. But as usual, Adrian was understanding of her husband, she sympathized with him and tried to comfort him in this crucial time.

Michael was trying to be calm about the situation. He went down to the Department of Labor to try to collect unemployment salary, while he searched for a job. Every day Michael would get up early in the morning and drive around searching for any kind of lead that would help him find a job. He would spend the entire day filling out forms in hope of soon receiving a job to support his family. Weeks had gone by and Michael still was unable to find a job. Things didn't seem to be going his way. He was concerned about not having a job because of his family. He wanted to be the provider. But this time, he was unable to do so.

The weeks had escalated to months and he still was without a job. During this period, the bills were piling up, his rent was paid every month through the little money that he was receiving from the Department of Labor. But that money wasn't enough to pay for the other bills. He tried to ensure that they at least had a place to lay their heads. With the money that was left over, Adrian would assure that food was always in their home. The couple had gone from bad times, to good times and now they found themselves back to where they started. Michael was trying to figure out a way to bring in some money for his family.

8

Now in December of 1993, Michael was not able to buy any Christmas gifts for Adrian or for Montel. He was almost coming into a desperate situation. He called Roger, in hope of him lending him some money for the holidays. Roger informed Michael of the fact that he was not working as well. Michael was running out of options. Roger sensed a urge of emergency in Michael's voice. He started to think of ways to help Michael, he felt badly that he was not able to help his dear friend in his time of need. So, Roger suggested that they meet somewhere in private so they could talk. Roger informed Michael that he had a way for them to get some money.

On December 20th, they met at a local bar, which they left to go for a ride in Roger's car. Roger informed Michael of his plan to rob a store. Michael did not agree with Roger's plan, but he did tell him that he would need to think about it and consider it, because of his current situation. He needed money in the worst way. Roger's plan to rob a store was something he had planned for quite awhile but he never told a soul.

After two days of thinking, Michael finally agreed to get in on Roger's scheme. Michael was skeptical about doing this, but felt it was necessary for the benefit of his family. Roger's plan called for them to rob a store on the 24th of December, but Michael wanted it to be on the 23rd. He wanted to buy his family gifts on the 24th with the money he was hoping to have after robbing the store.

On the evening of December 23rd, Michael and Roger headed to the store located on the corner of Albany avenue and Crown street. This was a little convenience store that the entire neighborhood shopped at. Local people would buy groceries from this store on a regular basis. Roger was very familiar with this store, he would see the amount of people that would enter it on a daily basis. He figured this would be a good location to rob, due to the fact that the money would be right. Both men drove to the location and waited until no one was inside the store. They only wanted to get to the register. They were not trying to hurt any bystander. At the first chance that they received to enter the store without any one being in there, they took it. They went into the store wearing masks, to hide their identity. They were successful in their quest. They were able to come out with 5,000 dollars, which was shared evenly between both men.

Michael got his wish and he was able to provide gifts for his family this Christmas. He bought his son many gifts that he was able to purchase from a Toys R Us toy store and for his wife he bought a pendant that was made out of white gold. Michael also was able to catch up with some of his bills. His wife was curious as to how he was able to get that much in such a short period of time. But, she never questioned her husband because she had faith and trust in whatever he was doing or was involved in. Her husband told her that he had borrowed the money from Roger, his old time friend.

After her husband informed her of how he got the money, Adrian was no longer worried but now wondered how her husband was going to be able to pay off all the money he had borrowed from Roger. Adrian believed that it was going to be difficult to pay him back, especially now that her husband did not have a job or a steady income coming in.

Both men were happy to have successfully burglarized the store, so, they came up with another idea to burglarize once again. But this time they wanted more money. Instead of going after a store, they decided to move up to robbing a check cashing place. This time they figured they had to put more time and dedication into it, if they wanted to be successful.

This time, they got another friend involved in their plan to rob a check cashing place. They first got a map of the location they were going to rob. They were precise in finding out the locations for each and every one of their alarm systems, along with cameras. Once they had all the details of the locations, they began to use everyone's skills, to facilitate the robbery.

Michael was familiar with disarming alarms. Basically he was familiar with security systems and due to this, he was responsible in ensuring that the whole alarm system, along with the camera system were disconnected. He disconnected every single one of them. This was made easier by the map provided to them by their third partner. Roger was responsible for creating the explosives necessary for entrance into the safe-deposit box. They were to blow the safe open to have access to the money.

The third party who was responsible for the acquisition of the map, was also responsible for positioning himself in a location close enough to collect the money and leave the scene of the crime. The robbery took place at night. They did not want anyone in the bank, because once again, they did not want to worry about hurting any innocent bystander. The robbery was executed to perfection. They were able to get in and out of the check cashing store without any traces of themselves left behind. They had now successfully robbed two different locations in a span of two weeks. This time they were able to get sixty thousand. This money was divided equally into three parts. Each man received twenty thousand dollars.

With this money, Michael was able to plan to buy a house for his family. He now didn't have to worry about expenses, because all of his bills were being paid now. Things seemed to be going their way once again. Michael was beginning to live a life he could only have imagined before. He had resorted to stealing, something his family would disapprove of but on the positive side, he now had the money, he could only have dreamed of having before. He found himself having not to worry about any bills. He was able to provide his family with all the luxuries he never had. He was beginning to enjoy this lifestyle, but he knew that it would only be a matter of time before the money he had stolen ran out on him. But he was enjoying the fact that he was getting away with a crime. At this time, he felt as if he was above the law. He did not believe that anyone could stop him. Adrian continued to stand by Michael, even though she disagreed with his new way of providing for the family.

   Michael couldn't stand the fact that he had lied to Adrian, so, he had confessed to her and told her the truth. It was painful to him to be doing what he was doing, but it was more painful to him to know that he had lied to her by telling her that he had borrowed the money from Roger. At the other end Adrian was disappointed to know that Michael had resorted to stealing, but was more disappointed to know that her husband had lied to her. He had promised her that he would never do such a thing as lie to her again, but he never gave her any guarantees as to whether or not he would steal again. Adrian did not agree with his new way of providing for his family, but she understood the predicament they were found in and she understood that they needed the money in the worst way. So, she promised not to get involved in any of her husband's doings. But she also promised to stand by him on whatever decisions he chose.

9

After feeling a sense of security in his relationship, Michael once again made preparations, along with Roger and Terrell to rob yet another location. The other two agreed to the idea, for they enjoyed the money as much as Michael did. They felt invincible, due to the fact that they did not get caught in their two previous attempts. In this third attempt, they planned to use the same format, Michael would once again be responsible for disarming the bank's alarm, along with any other security system and cameras. Roger's responsibility would be the explosives, and Terrell would be the driver. Terrell was to stay in the car while Michael and Roger went in and got the money.

This robbery would take more time to complete because it took more preparations due to the fact that it was a bank. They expected security to be more hectic at the bank. They would go to the bank and try to grasp as much information as possible. Trying to find out about the security system. How many cops it has at the time it closes, the time individuals working there went home what time they returned in the morning. They needed to know where the money is stocked up, what day the money will be picked up from the bank and so forth. . . .

After gathering all of this information, the men were ready for their next heist. They headed out to the bank, and upon arrival, Roger immediately headed toward the back of the bank where he had set up the explosives that would allow them to enter the bank. Prior to setting the explosives, Michael ensured that all of the alarms that would ordinarily sound off were disarmed. After signals from Michael, Roger set the explosives off. The back of the bank was open and no alarm had gone off. The men knew that they did not have that much time to accomplish what they had set out to do. So, they proceeded with the plan and they headed toward the safe. This is where Michael used some of the skills that he had learned while in the military. He was successful in opening the safe and proceeded by putting the money in the bag that he and Roger had taken with them inside of the bank. They took as much money that their bags would allow. They were once again successful in robbing a location, in a span of only three months. They headed outside where Terrell was waiting; they got into the car and drove off.

10

Michael and his friends were so good at what they were doing, that the city of New York had assigned a few detectives to the case. They were puzzled as to how anyone was successful in robbing this bank, without leaving any trace or clues as to who was responsible for the crime. At this time they had not linked the bank robbery to any other crime, because they were just at the beginning stages of the investigation. The lead detective for this case was a man by the name of Mark Johnson. He had been a detective for approximately twenty-seven years; the city was relying heavily on his experience to capture the individual or individuals responsible for the robbery. People believed that if anyone was capable of solving this case, he would be the one to do it.

The media started to get involved by covering details about the robbery that had taken place in the past month. That is how Michael and his accomplices were able to find out that the city had assigned a detective to solve the robbery case. Adrian was the one who had told Michael. She was watching the news when they reported about the robbery.

At the time of hearing the news, Adrian became scared and skeptical, she was afraid for her husband. She did not want him to risk going to jail. She was afraid that she would not be able to deal with the experience of Michael going to jail for a second time around, because she was unable to deal with it the first time. When he had spent some time in the military jail, she had missed him a great deal. She knew that if he got caught this time around, for stealing money from a bank, he would have to do years in a state prison.

She also knew that his credibility would be destroyed. She thought that after finding out that he had robbed a bank, everyone would begin to doubt his innocence while in the brig. People would begin to think that the crime he had claimed not to have had committed was actually his doing.

Adrian could not beat the idea of seeing her husband sent to prison, so she tried to rationalize with him. He promised her that he would take it easy for awhile. Even though he loved the money he was receiving from committing these crimes, he knew he loved Adrian even more. So, he decided not to take the risk of getting caught. He complied with Adrian's wish and started to stay home with his family. They had enough money to last them for awhile anyway. They had stolen one and a half million dollars from the bank, which they had shared evenly once again. Each man received half of a million dollars.

In an effort to help her husband, Adrian returned back to work. She was able to find a job as a financial analyst. While she worked, Michael stayed home watching their little boy. He enjoyed every minute that he was able to spend with his son. He would stay home, thinking of how much his wife loved him, and that after all his up and downs, she'd stayed by his side. She'd made the sacrifice of going out into the job market and finding herself a job. She found herself being the family provider.

A responsibility Michael had wanted to maintain all of his life, but he coped with this feeling during these times since he had no choice. He felt guilty and badly to know that he was not providing his family with their needs. But Michael accepted his new role, as he was also proud of his wife, knowing that she would go to the extremes to save their family. She did all of this because of her love for her husband. She believed that as long as she was bringing home money, he would not have the need or the want to go out and steal. Michael was fully aware of his wife's doing. He wanted to show her his appreciation for her efforts. Adrian did not need her husband to show his appreciation, she knew that her husband loved her as much as she loved him, and that's all that mattered to her. She did not care about what she had to do to maintain her marriage. She was truly a good woman, she stayed with her man throughout all this turmoil.

Months went by, and Adrian was still the only provider. She would come home to a cooked meal that her husband had prepared for her. Michael would cook and take care of all the household chores, while his lady was at work. During this time, Michael still found the time to search for a job. Adrian appreciated all of her husband's work. She would come home to a clean house and, basically she had nothing to do, because her husband took care of everything. Adrian would spend some quality time with her husband and son.

Before they knew it, Michael found himself a job. There were now two sources of income, which made it easier for them to put some of the money that Michael had stolen into the bank. They gradually put a certain amount in the account on a weekly basis. They tried to only put in a small amount to ensure that no one would become suspicious of them. The bank account was in Adrian's name. Without realizing it, Adrian had found herself involved in her husband's crimes. She was actually an accomplice now.

11

Detective Mark Johnson was a devoted husband and father. He had two kids of his own. But, when he was not involved with his family, he would be found at the precinct solving cases. He was a man who loved his job. He would put in long hours at work each and every day of the week. At work, people were not too fond of him, because of his strict and business-like attitude. But, they respected him because he went about his job in the correct way of conducting business. He did not care about who liked him or not, his only concern was performing the job to the best of his ability. That was the only way he knew how to perform his duty. After twenty-seven years of service, there were not too many things he had not experienced. He knew the tricks of the trade. The in's and out's. He did not believe that anyone could outsmart him when it came to his job.

After taking this case, he was confused as to how the individuals managed to rob the bank without leaving any traces behind. He figured he was dealing with experts, without having any clues as to who, or how many individuals were involved. He just knew it was not the work of a single individual because of the manner in which the robbery was conducted.

Detective Johnson went around the location, where the crime had occurred and started inquiring about it. He went to stores, parks, and he even knocked on people's doors, but to his surprise, no one managed to know anything about the robbery. The detective found himself at a standstill situation, for he hadn't managed to get any information that would link or lead him to anyone.

The three individuals who conducted the crimes managed to do a good job, in not helping the detectives find any clues. Days started turning into weeks, and Detective Johnson still didn't have any clues that would help him solve any of the crimes. He was puzzled; he wanted to nail the individuals who committed the crimes. At the same time, he felt as if he could congratulate them for doing an astounding job in not leaving any traces behind. This was a sarcastic thought. He couldn't understand how anyone could commit what he almost considered to be a perfect crime. The only thing short of making this crime perfect was the fact that he believed he would eventually capture the individuals responsible for it. Even though he was not close to solving this case, he refused to give up. Through hard work, Mr. Johnson knew that this case would come to an end. Patience was not Johnson's strongest suit, but he had no choice but to be patient if he hoped to ever solve this case.

To date, this was the hardest case he had encountered in his tenure as a detective. He had managed to solve an undisclosed number of cases, without any major set backs. That's why he was assigned to this case. It seemed as if the robbers managed to outsmart him this time around. For awhile, he contemplated retirement, but his family did not think that he should retire under the conditions that he spoke of. They believed that he should retire under his conditions and not allow a case to lead him in that direction. His family never knew him to be a quitter, so they did not want him to retire quitting. His family encouraged him to stay and continue to pursue the criminals who had committed this bank robbery. With his family support, Detective Johnson started to put in long hours, in pursuit of the unknown robbers.

On the eve of May 25, 1994, Detective Johnson received something he believed to be a lead from an unknown source. Since he had nothing else to go by, he decided to look into it. The unknown individual had told the police that he saw two men rob a bank. He told them that he did not get the chance to see their faces because both men had masks on and they also had weapons, which made it harder for anyone to get any descriptions of them. The man was able to give the detectives what he believed to be the height and weight of the two individuals believed to be the robbers.

This information was not a lot to go by, but they figured since they had nothing else, it was worth a try in pursuing their first lead. This lead was only the first of many to come into the precinct, and the detective started to feel more optimistic about eventually bringing someone to justice for the committed crimes.

Another lead came in and it was the description of a car, which they believed would make it easier for them to finally get a positive trace. So, after finding the plate number believed to be that of the getaway car in the robbery, Detective Johnson started to follow up on it. He hoped to see if he could get anymore information that would eventually lead him to these individuals, or any other person involved in this crime. The owner of the vehicle was a man by the name of Victor Williams, he was self-employed. He had an office where he performed repairs on televisions and VCR's. The cops conducted an investigation and they concluded that Mr. Williams did own this store and that he had been a popular figure in his neighborhood. People were surprised to see cops come into Mr. William's shop for any reason.

Detective Johnson did not see a reason for this man robbing the bank, since, he was a man that seemed to be well-off financially. But at the same time, he did not want to take anything for granted. So, he continued to conduct the investigation into the bank robbery. Detective Johnson ordered Victor Williams to be brought into the precinct for questioning. During the process of intense questioning, he came to the realization that this man had nothing to do with this crime and was not guilty. Mr. Williams had an account of when and where he was at the time of this crime. Luckily for him, other people were able to attest to his whereabouts during this period of time.

Mr. Williams was set free to go home and resume his life, he was assured that they would not be bringing him back into the precinct for any further questioning. The detectives apologized for their mistake and told him that they were only doing their jobs. It was a lead that they had to follow and they did. He was told that he was no longer a suspect, and that they were going to look into other venues. Mr. Williams was a very good man. He accepted their apologies and told them not to worry about the mishap; he said that mistakes do happen and this one happens to be one of them. The detectives were so glad that they got a chance to work with Mr. Williams; as opposed to having another individual who might not have been that forgiving of their huge mistake.

Even though they were not able to arrest anyone for the robberies, they were at least able to arrest someone for conspiracy. It happens that the unknown individual who had called in regards to the crime, had lied about what he claimed he had seen. He did not see anyone going into any bank, he had lied, because he wanted to collect the reward money offered to anyone who could help in the capturing of any of the criminals involved in the robbery. Detective Williams was able to find out that this unknown individual was lying because he was not consistent in his statements. He had first accounted for not knowing how the two robbers looked because of them wearing masks that made it hard for him to recognize them. But later in his statement, he told the detectives that they were both black and in that little piece of information, they were able to find an inconsistency with his story. The detectives continued to interrogate him. He finally gave in and told them the truth, that he had lied to cash in on some money. The detective were so involved in this case, that they were aggravated by this individual's doing.

They knew that this case was giving them a hard time as it was, so to have an individual try to divert them from getting any closer to solving this case was infuriating. They charged him with as many charges as they possibly could, to make an example out of him. They wanted to encourage people not to lie to get money, especially when it deals with someone's innocence. In this case, Mr. Williams's innocence had been on the line. Mr. Williams was delighted to hear of the news that the person responsible for him being taken in for interrogation was arrested for conspiracy.

But now, Detective Johnson was back to where he first started, without any clues, or any optimism as to finding the guilty parties anytime soon. He continued his pursuit though. He started to follow other leads, but without any luck.

12

Meanwhile, Michael was back at home relaxing and he along with his wife continued to follow the case to see if they were getting any closer to solving it. Michael was certain that they would never figure this case out, unless, he or his partners opened their mouths. The person he was worried about was Adrian. Not because of her knowing the truth, but because he hated to see her involved in his wrong doing. She was concerned about her husband's well being, even though he assured her that everything would be alright. She continued to provide for her family, even though her husband had found himself a job. His job wasn't a great one but it was good enough to keep him busy and out of trouble.

Adrian still found herself in a position where she was afraid to even see her husband step out of the house, in fear of a cop arresting him. But, in time, she began to feel more at ease to see her husband in public, as the fear of him getting caught gradually decreased as time went on. She felt more confident as the media decreased their covering of the bank robbery. Adrian thought that because she was not hearing anymore things in regard to the crime, that the detective had stopped pursuing the robbers. Little did she know, that there was a persistent detective still on the case. Detective Johnson never quit in his quest to catch these men or women. Even though this crime was not publicized on television as it once was, he still continued to pursue it. In a way he felt less pressured to find the guilty parties, because the media was not covering the case as much as they once did. So now, he only had to focus on the crime and not on the media or anyone else.

Meanwhile at home, Roger Henderson could be found enjoying his money. He made the best of his situation. He invested some of the money and luckily for him, he was able to make more money. The shares he had purchased on the Wall Street Stock Exchange had increased. So, he had profited from his investments. He was familiar with stocks, but he also had a whole lot of luck on his side. He made the right decision this time for a change in his life.

Like Michael, he was living the luxurious life. He bought a house with a swimming pool; he had four cars, and provided himself with everything possible. Everything seemed to be going smoothly for these two men.

But unlike them, Terrell was not that lucky. He did not make good use of his money. He got involved in using some heavy drugs, a dependency he was able to afford with the money he received from the robberies. But, he was too dependent on these drugs, to the point that he lost track of time. He would purchase his drugs on a everyday basis.

At first, he started using marijuana, which was a drug that everyone around him seemed to be using. But, this drug was not providing him with the effects he was looking for. So later, he escalated to trying out other drugs. He started to feel comfortable with cocaine, a drug he felt was strong enough to give him the effects he was seeking. Little did he know, that in time, he would be doing things he would not be able to acknowledge. It was to the point where Michael and Roger did not want anything to do with him, but, they had no choice but to look out for him. They feared that eventually, he would tell someone of their wrongdoings. Both men, kept a close eye on Terrell.

Terrell kept his mouth shut, he did not tell anyone about the robberies. He was too focused on the drugs to remember anything about the crimes. It was more as if he would block it out of his mind. Cocaine was the only thing he wanted to think about. As long as there were drugs, he was happy.

Time went on and Terrell continued to keep his silence. It was a sign of relief for the other two men. There were times when Michael and Roger would think of ways to ensure that Terrell maintained his silence. At times Roger would come up with the idea of killing Terrell, but Michael did not see the need for that. Michael wanted to see first if Terrell would attempt to say anything, but as time went on, Terrell still did not mention anything in regards to the crimes. Michael saw it as good sign, because killing his friend was the last thing that he wanted to do. Michael convinced Roger not to kill Terrell. Roger wanted to do it because he did not want to take any chances of getting caught by the police. He was enjoying his life too much to have an individual destroy his hard work. He loved being at the top, having money, luxury cars, and most of all he loved his independence. Roger agreed to take it easy, but warned Michael that he only needed to hear once that Terrell opened his mouth, and he would then take action. Michael saw that as a fair deal, so both men agreed on it.

As weeks went by and Terrell continued to maintain his silence, his life was not at stake when it came to Roger. He would buy his drugs, then he would head home and make use of them. The neighborhood that he happened to be living in was corrupted with drugs. It was like a war zone. Everyone either sold or used drugs. On occasion, the police department would send some policemen to try to control the trafficking of drugs in this neighborhood. The policemen seemed to be there more for show than for protection. Even though there were cops on occasion in Terrell's neighborhood, people still knew that they had no intentions of making any serious attempts to stop the flow of drugs into the neighborhood. Things were so bad, that some parents were afraid of sending their kids outside, just to even play. To these parents, it did not matter what time was, they only cared about their kids' safety. They were fearful of sending their children outside and not getting the chance to ever see them again. Every time they saw their kids, it was as if it was going to be their last.

13

On July 3, 1994, Terrell was arrested for the purchase of drugs. At the time, it seemed as if it was only a random bust. But as time went on and more investigation took place, the cops begun to be curious as to how he was able to purchase the amount of drugs that he did on a regular basis. Things did not seem to be going alright for Terrell. He was at risk of being jailed for a long period of time, along with him incriminating his other two friends. He was in constant fear of his partners because they had already warned him. In this case, it was Roger more so than Michael. Roger was the one that was willing to kill Terrell if he ever was to talk about the robberies.

Well, during the investigation, the detectives continued to be persistent in their questioning of Terrell, they knew that he was hiding something. They were hoping that it had to do with the robberies because this was a case that they were working on so hard without any success. After days of interrogation, Terrell gave in. He was beginning to feel the effects of not using drugs for those few days. He was desperate. He was willing to do anything in hopes of getting some drugs to satisfy his thirst for them. The detectives played a trick on him, they told him that they were willing to give him some drugs if he could only speak of what he knew. They went so far as showing him some drugs in hope of convincing him. To their surprise, it worked. He confessed to the crimes, but he ensured that he did not mention anything that would incriminate his other two partners. To Detective Johnson this was a huge surprise because Terrell did not only admit to the bank robbery but also to the other two crimes they had committed.

The word got out on the street that Terrell was involved in the bank robbery along with two other crimes, and to Michael and Roger this was not good news. They were desperate to find out what it was that Terrell had said about the robberies. This whole thing was a police plot in hopes of having the other parties involved come forward and confess to the robberies. These two men were more concerned about Terrell breaking down and confessing to the entire truth and letting the detectives know that they were the other two men that had helped him with the robberies.

Once again, Michael was concerned about his wife Adrian. She began to get terrified because she was in fear of having her husband arrested. She prayed and hoped that everything would eventually work out. Michael, the strong-minded man that he was, assured her once again, that everything would eventually work out. She believed in her husband and stood by him throughout his ordeal. Michael was very appreciative of his wife. On the other side, Roger was freaking out, he told Michael that he had warned him about Terrell and that they should act now on their plan to kill Terrell. This was to be a difficult quest, since Terrell had detectives watching over him. They knew that eventually they would catch the other parties involved. That's why, they put a 24-hour watch on Terrell, to ensure his safety.

People found it hard to believe that Terrell had committed these crimes and that even though he was accused of committing them, he was still released from prison and sent home. All of this was odd, but it was part of the plan to eventually catch the other robbers. All of this was ordered by Detective Johnson. He began to be more optimistic about eventually arresting the guilty parties soon. He began to put more hours in, hoping he soon would be bringing the guilty parties into the judicial system and finally bringing this case to an end.

This case seemed to have become an obsession for Detective Johnson because of the hours that he would constantly put in each and every day at the precinct. Detective Johnson began to go into Terrell's records, he was hoping to find something that would eventually put this case to a close. He wanted to know of all the individuals who were close to him.

After an intense search, he found out that the person or friends closest to him were Michael and Roger. Even though he had nothing on these two men, he saw it suitable to bring these two men in for questioning.

First it was Michael, this did not go well with Adrian. She was present when the detective came over and took him in for questioning. She was a nervous wreck. Detective Johnson went into Michael's past history and to his surprise found the records of him spending time in the brig but couldn't use that against him because he knew that the military uses its own judicial system instead of the civilian way. Apart from his military past experience, the detective found nothing he believed to incriminate this man. He saw him as a hard working family man. A man who was devoted to his family, who provided to the best of his ability. He saw a younger image of himself in Michael.

Even though he did not see anything that would incriminate Michael at the time, he still had to continue his investigation of him, he just had an investigative mind. He still believed that even though someone may seem innocent doesn't necessarily mean that the individual is innocent. So, he assigned a detective to keep a very close eye on Michael, he wanted to know of his every move around the clock.

After Michael was questioned by Detective Johnson, Roger was brought in for questioning. His interrogation did not go well with the dectective because of his prior criminal record. They automatically were biased toward him, even before they questioned him about this present crime. After looking through his records, they realized that he had spent some time in jail, for robbing a retail store and later he was arrested for exploding a financial institution while in the military. They automatically saw him as a potential lead to solving this case. He went to the top of their list as a primary suspect. They were trying to see if they could link the explosives he had used in the military to explode that financial institution and the bomb that was later used on the bank.

Roger did not help his case too much, because even though he did not incriminate himself while being interrogated, he was not helpful to the detectives. He showed a dislike toward the judicial system and he also disrespected all of the detectives while being questioned. It was as if he had something against them. The detectives did not take this lightly. While at the precinct, the detectives made life difficult for Roger because of the way he had behaved towards them. They kept him at the precinct for long hours; they interrogated him continuously.

After those long hours of interrogations, the detectives were unable to find anything that they believed to incriminate Roger of the crimes, but they saw it suitable to have someone follow his every move just like they had ordered someone to do with Michael.

Unlike his feelings of Michael, Mr. Johnson did not have good instincts of Roger. He saw Roger as a man capable of committing any crime, he saw him as dangerous and desperate. His intuition kept him believing that Roger had something to do with the bank robbery crime. His belief was that Roger would be the one that would lead him to finally solving this case.

After being interrogated, Roger and Michael saw each other to discuss their next move. Roger was still with the idea of killing Terrell, it was as if he was obsessed with the idea of seeing Terrell dead. But he did not see it that way, he believed that it was more a sense of urgency on his behalf. He just did not want to put his life in the hands of Terrell and risk it by having him tell the police everything that had happened. Michael was more at ease with the situation, he did not want to see Terrell tell the detectives what he knew but he was preparing himself for the unexpected. He believed that if Terrell opened his mouth and told the authorities of the crimes, that they still had a chance of getting away with it because they did not think that a jury would believe the story of an unreliable source. That is what Michael considered Terrell, he knew that while under those conditions, it was almost impossible for him to be a good witness to support the state's case because of his inability to sound believable. Detective Johnson knew it as well. He knew that Terrell would not be a good witness to the court because of his unstableness, but he believed that he was part of the clue to eventually solving this case. Detective Johnson believed Terrell's story, there was a bit of truthfulness to what he was saying.

After fully discussing their next move, Michael and Roger figured that it would be in their best interest to maintain a low profile of themselves, but at the same time to not change anything that they have been doing for the past few months. They did not want to make anyone suspicious of them. Michael thought that since they had been meeting each other on a regular basis, it made no sense to change their routine because it would give Detective Johnson along with the rest of the detectives assigned to the case, a chance to become more suspicious of them. Michael did not want to give Detective Johnson the benefit of the doubt. He believed that as long as Roger and he did the right thing, eventually Detective Johnson would have no option but to give up on them and either give up on the case or pursue someone else as their suspect.

Little did they know that Detective Johnson had made a vow to his family to pursue this case regardless of how long it took him to find the guilty parties involved. Detective Johnson, along with the other detectives assigned to this case continued to keep a close eye on Michael and Roger to see if they can get any closer to finally putting an end to this case. Months went by and neither Michael nor Roger would lead any of the detectives to any clues that would help solve this case. The other detectives were beginning to give up on Michael and Roger, they wanted Detective Johnson to give up on these guys and start pursuing other people. They saw Michael and Roger as a deadend. After a few months of around the clock watch on Michael and Roger, Detective Johnson was too stubborn to give up on these two guys, especially Roger.

He continued his pursuit, at the same time, he continued to keep a close eye on Terrell's progress. For the past few months Terrell was institutionalized in a drug rehabilitation center. Detective Johnson believed that once he had recovered, Terrell could get less time in jail for confessing to the robberies and he could also be more believable in a court room once he was fully clean of drug use.

The system had brainwashed Terrell's thinking completely. They had him believing that the best thing for him to do was to tell them everything that he knew about the robberies. Detective Johnson found this time as being the appropriate time to ask questions because he had been sober for quite a while, since he had just been released from the rehabilitation center. The doctors did not want the detectives to pressure Terrell because they feared that he may resort back to taking drugs if he found the situation to be too hectic. They feared that he may use drugs again as a scapegoat. Mr. Johnson promised to be diligent in his quest to get answers from Terrell. He would visit Terrell on a regular basis to check on his progress and see if he was willing to part with some extra information.

14

Two weeks after returning home, Roger paid Terrell a visit. He was very disappointed in Terrell for opening his mouth, but at the same time thankful to know that he had enough sense not to incriminate his other two partners in the crime. These two men had a very long and intense conversation. This is where Roger had informed him that if he ever were to mention anything in regards to these crimes to the police that he would personally kill him. This did not go well with Terrell. He did not know how to take this piece of information. Terrell had just returned from rehab, so he was not fully recovered and he knew that this sickness was going to be a daily fight for him, just like he was informed at the center.

The next day after Roger visited Terrell, Detective Johnson went over to Terrell's house to pay him his regular visit and to his surprise, he found Terrell dead. It seemed that Terrell had taken his own life in fear of what Roger had told him. Terrell had hung himself. This was not good news to Detective Johnson's ear. He was very disappointed because this was supposed to be his main lead in solving this case. Detective Johnson was unsure as to the reason why he had taken his life. He thought that Terrell was stable enough not to take his life away. He believed him to be okay since he had just paid him a visit a few days prior.

News had gotten back to Michael that Terrell was dead. Michael's first thought was that Roger had killed him. He had tried to get in contact with Roger to ask him why did he kill Terrell after he had promised that he would not? After finally getting in contact with Roger, Michael asked why did he kill Terrell after having a discussion with him, and promising him that he would not kill him? Roger was shocked to hear of the news of Terrell's death. He told Michael that he had nothing to do with his death. Michael did not believe him because he knew that Roger had just paid their old friend a visit. Michael thought that the killing occurred when Roger had gone over to Terrell's house.

After discussing the matter with Roger, he started to believe that Roger had not killed Terrell. The news was made more clear to Michael by the television news who had informed the world that the suspected bank robber had taken his own life away.

Michael was saddened to know of Terrell's death, but happy to know that Roger was not responsible for his death.

After conducting a small investigation of Terrell's death Detective Johnson came to find out that Roger had paid him a visit the day before he had killed himself. That news did not go well with the detective, they wanted to know the reason for Roger's visit and to also find out if Roger was the one responsible for his death. Roger knew that his timing was bad and that he was going to be harassed by the detectives. Especially Detective Johnson, who was looking for any piece of evidence that would incriminate Roger to the crime.

Michael did not like Detective Johnson's antics, he thought that the detective was harassing Roger. So, he made an appointment to meet with Mr. Johnson. That's when he informed him of his feelings. Detective Johnson did not like the fact that Michael was questioning him about the way that he was performing his job. The conversation got intense to where both men started to lose all the respect that they seemed to have for one another. Detective Johnson now started to believe that maybe Michael had something to do with this crime because he did not see any other reason for anyone defending someone of any crime to the extent that Michael was trying to help Roger. Michael was getting so irritated to the point where he felt incline to rob a bank to show this detective that he could do it again without getting caught again.

As the argument continued to progress, Detective Johnson informed Michael that he believed that he and his friend Roger were the other two parties involved in the robbery. To Detective Johnson's surprise, Michael confessed to him that he was the one who had robbed the bank along with the other two locations, just like Terrell had told him. This is how upset Michael was, to the point where he had something to prove to the detective. The only reason for his confession is because he knew that Detective Johnson could not do anything with this information because if it came down to going to court for this case, Michael would not admit to committing any of these crimes and it will be Detective Johnson's word against his word in the courtroom. Michael knew exactly what he was doing. Detective Johnson also knew that even though Michael had confessed to him that he could not do anything with that information because he had no other proof or evidence against him.

15

Two months later, Michael found himself plotting another robbery. He had informed Roger and he was once again willing to go through with this next plan. The only thing they needed this time was two other partners. Michael took care of that. He informed two of his ex-coworkers from the alarm shop. He figured they were desperate for the money since they too had lost their jobs and they also had a hard time finding another one. Michael also wanted them involved because they were also familiar with alarm and camera systems which could help.

All four men got together in preparation for their next robbery. The other two men were really anxious and willing. Michael liked that in them, but also informed them to be patient if they wanted to be successful in this robbery.

This robbery was something that Michael worked extra hard at because he really wanted to succeed at proving a point to the detective; that some one could actually commit wrong and get away with it. This was Michael's stubborn side talking, a side that Detective Johnson brought out of him.

All four men started to conduct research on their plan. They selected a location which they believed they would be more successful at robbing. They later went about finding out about the security installed in the bank. They visited the bank on a regular basis to inquire about all the details necessary to make this robbery successful.

All of their work did not go unnoticed, Detective Johnson was following their every move. He had an idea as to what they were planning to do next. So, he kept his watchful eyes on them while they continued their plan. Detective

Johnson started to go into the records of the other two men. He wanted to know everything there was to know about them, in hopes of finding some helpful clues. He found out that both of these individuals had prior records and they were dangerous, but that they had held a job for a while, only to lose them to a fire.

After weeks of following their every move and nothing had been done, Detective Johnson scheduled to meet with Michael because he wanted to inform him that he knew about their next plan. So on the eve of June 7, 1995, Michael and Detective Johnson met. This is the time when they went into a lengthy conversation.

They met at a restaurant, where they ordered coffee. Both men started talking and this is when Detective Johnson informed Michael that he knew of their next move. Michael did not seem surprised because he was expecting the detective to keep a watchful eye on them. At this time Michael told the detective so what if he knew that they were going to rob a bank? He told the detective that even though he knew of their plan, he was not going to stop them from accomplishing their goal. Detective Johnson told Michael that if he continued with his intentions to rob that bank, he was going to have to take some action. Even if it would take killing him, he was going to do it because it was part of his job to stop him from robbing the bank.

Michael then informed him that he needed to do what was best for him, because he was going to still continue with his plan of robbing the bank, and if he got in his way he was going to have to take some action. That being killing him. He said he was determined to get away with this crime and he had no intentions of going back to any kind of prison.

Detective Johnson asked Michael of his family and if he was willing to leave them behind? Michael informed the detective that they had nothing to do with what they were talking about and that he was determined to go through with his intentions and that his family understood. He informed him that even if he was to be killed, at least they would be well taken care of financially. Both men left the conversation firm on what they believed, they actually shook hands at the end of their meeting and told each other that the best man will win. This whole case turned out to be like a personal vendetta between these two men. They were both stubborn and determined to get what they wanted.

Both men left the restaurant with a better understanding of where each one of them stood. Even though Detective Johnson knew of Michael's intentions of robbing the bank on the Fourth of July, he continued to keep a watchful eye on him on a daily basis. Detective Johnson was up for the task, he personally followed Michael's every move.

At the other side of the spectrum, Michael was continuing with his plan to rob the bank on Independence Day. He determined to conduct this plan to perfection. After all of the preparations for the robbery, he knew that Detective Johnson was keeping a close eye on him. So, he diverted the plan a little. He planned not to be at the scene of the crime and get Detective Johnson's attention while his partners were conducting the robbery.

First; Michael built an electronic device that would automatically send a signal to his friends while he was at a different location. This device was so small, Michael could place it on his key chain. Upon pressing a button, it would immediately send a signal to inform them that everything was clear and that they could go ahead with the plan of robbing the bank. They tried this device on many different occasions, to ensure that it worked and it did work every single time.

One of the individuals that Michael worked with, named Peter, stole a jeep which was to be used for the robbery. That way the car couldn't be traced back to them. Peter was fully responsible for driving them to and from the scene of the robbery.

Michael's other ex-coworker, whose name was Dontell, was to take Michael's place. He was responsible for the disarming of the alarm system and making the entrance to the bank as safe as possible. Dontell found this task to be easy since he had been dealing with security systems for most of his adult life. As usual, Roger's responsibility was to create the explosive necessary for entrance into the bank.

On the day that these individuals were to rob the bank, Detective Johnson showed up at Michael's home. He told him that he needed to talk to him. Michael was expecting him to show up at his home. That's why he did not include himself in the robbery. Detective Johnson thought that he outsmarted Michael this time because he figured if he spent the entire day with Michael it would prevent him from robbing the bank.

Both men headed toward a restaurant in Brooklyn. It was a local diner. Once again, they ordered coffee, it was approximately 12:15 P.M. in the afternoon. His partners were already set to carry out the plan, all they were waiting for was Michael's signal. Over at the diner Michael and Johnson talked over old matters. Detective Johnson was surprised to see Michael calm. He was anticipating Michael to be in a rush to leave since he had made plans to rob a bank on this day.

Detective Johnson while conversing with Michael sarcastically said to him, "I guess, I ruined your plans, right?" and Michael replied "No you have not, I am still going to carry it out." Then Detective Johnson said, "Not today my son, not today," and Michael replied "I guess not, ah!" Detective Johnson was puzzled because Michael was not giving him the replies that he wanted to hear from him. An hour passed and both men were still at the table conversing.

At approximately 1:30 in the afternoon, Michael pressed the button to his device to inform his buddies that it was time to execute their plan. Detective Johnson thought of it as being so strange to see Michael playing with his key chain, he actually thought that Michael was pressing the button to disarm a car. So, he really did not look too much into it. They continued talking as if nothing happened.

At the bank, all three men were executing the plan to perfection. Dontell was successful in disarming all of the alarms within the bank and Roger was also successful in making an easy entrance into the bank with his explosive. They immediately went over to the safe vault, where Dontell immediately proceeded to open it. He was successful and both men packed both bags with as much money as they possibly could get. They quickly headed outside where Peter was waiting with the jeep he had stolen. They quickly headed to where they had hidden another car to where they could switch and make it safer for them to return back to their neighborhood. Once again the plan worked to perfection. Michael had gotten his wish of outsmarting Detective Johnson.

Over at the diner, Detective Johnson was informed that the bank had been robbed and that someone had stolen over a million dollars. Michael saw when Mr. Johnson received the beep and immediately got on his phone to return the call. Michael saw that Detective Johnson had an amazed look, so, he automatically knew what the call was about.

At this point Michael asked him, did someone rob the bank? Michael knew that he had outsmarted this detective.

Detective Johnson was enraged to know of these happenings. He already knew by the look on his face that Michael had something to do with the robbery but could not do anything to him because he had the perfect alibi. He was *with* Detective Johnson. Detective Johnson acknowledged to Michael that he had done a good job, but he would still try to do something to get to the bottom of this mess. Detective Johnson concluded the meeting with Michael and headed to the bank that had been robbed.

On his way to the bank, Johnson started to think about the little device that Michael had pressed while they were at the restaurant and he started to think that must have been the time that Michael probably used to send a signal to his partners. This made Detective Johnson mad to know that he did not pay attention to that at the time that it happened.

Over at the house, Michael met with his three friends. This is where they celebrated their successful robbery. Michael was proud of the fact that he was able to accomplish his goal. Michael figured he got back at Detective Johnson and he promised never to indulge himself in that kind of lifestyle again.

Michael planned to use the money that he had saved along with his new wealth and open an alarm store where all four men could be involved in making legitimate money and building back a reputable reputation, by keeping up a legitimate place of business.

Detective Johnson was still amazed at how Michael sent a signal to alert his partners and he was still upset at the fact that he did not pay any attention at the time that it happened. Johnson was resilient in his pursuit. He did not want to get discouraged by what had happened. He was embarrassed, because he knew that Michael had planned to rob the bank on July fourth but he was still unable to stop him, so now, he found himself back to where he first started. He knows who did it but has no proof to indict the guilty party.

Michael was at home explaining his intentions to his wife. She was happy to know that her husband was promising her to leave that type of life behind. He also promised her that he would spend more time with her and their little boy. Michael also informed his wife that he had already found a location for his store. All he needed to do was finalize the deal. To prevent any hassles from the police, he had Adrian purchase the building that was going to be used to run the store. After a few weeks of negotiations, the deal was finalized and Michael had finally gotten his store. He was now to be his own boss. After the business got on its feet, Michael did not want Adrian to be working anymore. It took a while for the store to get up on its feet but it finally happened. The good thing about the store is that it gave an opportunity for all four men to get a new beginning to their lives. All four men were working and stable.

16

Six months after the store had opened, Detective Johnson went into the store and requested to talk to Michael. The other three men, along with Adrian were curious as to why he had gone into the store to see Michael. After seeing Michael, Detective Johnson approached him and asked him if it was possible for them to have a conversation in private. Both men went into one of the offices inside of the store. Detective Johnson informed him that he would not be pursuing him any longer because as far as he was concerned the case was closed. He explained to Michael that he did want to find the proof to incriminate him but that he no longer had the strength to want to pursue it. He had explained to him that he was going to retire, something he was going to do until this case had come up. He told him that the only reason he had not retired earlier was because he wanted to bring the bank robber into the judicial system and handed over their proper sentence. Johnson told Michael that he no longer needed to worry about him and he wished him well.

Michael did not understand why Detective Johnson would come over to wish him well. Johnson told Michael that he reminded him of himself because he was persistent and he went for what he believed and wanted. He admired that in an individual. He also told him that now that he was receiving his second chance in life, not to ruin it. To take care of his family and to do the right thing in life. Michael assured him that he did not need to worry about him ever leading that lifestyle again because he was set for life and he did not ever want to jeopardize his family's future ever again. Mr. Johnson told him that he hoped that he never resorted back to that life because if he did he would come out, out of retirement to arrest him and this time he would find the evidence to incriminate him.

Michael laughed at Mr. Johnson's remark but knew that he was speaking the truth. Michael apologized to Mr. Johnson for their previous meeting and told Mr. Johnson that he was a good man and that if he ever needed anything, to not hesitate in asking him for it. Mr. Johnson also thanked Michael and told him that he was a good man himself and to continue in the direction he was heading. Both men extended their arm and gave each other a firm handshake and wished each other good luck. Mr. Johnson then headed toward the exit.

As Mr. Johnson exited the store, Adrian immediately approached her husband to try to find out what had happened. Michael informed his wife that Mr. Johnson was retiring and that he had closed the book on the case and that they had nothing to worry about. That was a sign of relief for Adrian. They were finally going to be able to live the kind of life they wanted to live. They didn't have to worry any longer about the authorities or about any financial problem. They were pretty much set.

At this time Adrian and Michael gave each other a huge hug, Adrian then told her husband that "this is what she has always wanted, to have her husband next to her" and Michael let her know that everyone makes mistakes. It just happens that he made a few, but luckily for him, he was able to learn from them. Michael believed that he was truly lucky.

Michael then kissed his wife and looked into her eyes and let her know that everything was going to be alright, and he told her that "it's finally over."

Acknowledgments and "Thank You"

I would like to first and foremost thank God for his love and guidance. To my parents for their continued support and love. To my brother, Wegener Ervan, and sisters, Rebeca Xiomara and Leicest Dorsy, for their patience. Love you, too, Vielka Macia. To the three positive minds who helped me and influenced me into becoming the man that I am today, my uncles Fernando, Alfonso, and Octavio. Thank you for all the advice. To the rest of the family who showed and gave me all the love in the world. To my extended family, the Reids; and Everton, you are truly my brother and best friend. To Ms. Dawn Jordan for her unyielding belief in me and to my publishing company for the opportunity. Thank you to everyone who helped provide me with the time, confidence, and love to write this book.